GW00889122

Common Entrance Practice Exam Papers 13+

Science

Azhar Hussain

Avicenna Education ©

CONTENTS

INTRODUCTION

These practice papers have been designed to help parents, students and tutors get the best possible grades in the 13+ exams. Preparing for the 13+ can be very stressful, but there really is no need to panic. Knowing exactly what your child (or you!) will be tested on and practicing exam papers is the key to success.

ABOUT ME

I actually failed all of my entrance exams to grammar schools when I was 11 and so ended up at my local comprehensive school. I did quite well for my GCSE's and then went on to go to a grammar school for sixth form. I got accepted at Cambridge University to read Medicine, in which I received a First Class BSc. I then transferred to Oxford University to complete the rest of my degree. I am now currently working as a doctor in the Hammersmith Hospital in London and aspire to be a surgeon when I grow up!

Having tutored for the last 7 years, and sat more than 100 exams myself, I have realized the key to success is exam technique as much as it is about knowledge. My aim with these papers and answer guides is to develop an effective exam technique. Becoming familiar with the type of questions they ask and what the examiners are looking for is very important. Equally important is what they are not looking for! It is simply not enough to know your subject well, but rather, it is how well you know your subject for exams. The answer guides will talk you through the questions rather than simply state a right/wrong answer and help you build an effective technique.

If you have any questions or would like further advice or have found any inconsistencies in the books please feel free to email on
query@avicennaeducation.co.uk

GOOD LUCK!

SURNAME ………………………………… FIRST NAME …………………………………………

JUNIOR SCHOOL ……………………………… SENIOR SCHOOL………………………………………

Avicenna Education©

COMMON ENTRANCE EXAMINATION AT 13+

SCIENCE

BIOLOGY PRACTICE PAPER 1

Date…………………………………..

Please read the information below before the examination starts.

- The examination is 40 minutes long.

- All answers should be written on the question paper

- Answer **all** questions.

- Calculators are allowed and may be required.

1. Underline the option which best completes each of the following sentences:

(a) Methylene blue is used to stain

cytoplasm   cell membrane   nuclei   mitochondria

(b) Fish is a good source of

carbohydrate   protein   fibre   fat

(c) The chemical products of photosynthesis are

carbon dioxide and energy   glucose and oxygen

carbon dioxide and water   energy and oxygen

(d) Iodine solution can be used to test for

starch   glycogen   fat   water

(e) The name given to the cell when a sperm cell and an egg cell fuse is called

fertilization   gamete   zygote   fetus

(f) An example of a disease caused by a bacteria is

scurvy   athlete's foot   influenza   tuberculosis

(g) The surface area of the lungs is increased by the presence of

villi   cilia   alveoli   flagellum

(h) Both plants and animals

photosynthesize   respire   have blood   breathe

(i) An example of discontinuous variation is

height   blood group   weight   hair length

(9)

2. The diagram below shows a leaf cell from a plant:

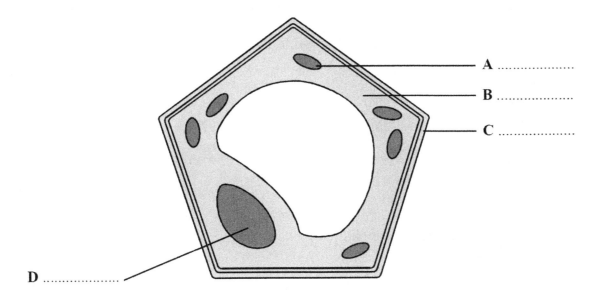

(a) From the list below label the diagram **A - D**

nucleus	**cytoplasm**	**chloroplast**	**ribosome**
vacuole	**cell membrane**	**cell wall**	**cilia**

(4)

(b) From the same list above, name two parts of a plant cell which are **NOT** found in animal cells.

cell part 1 ....

cell part 2 .... (2)

(c) Both plant cells and animal cells have specific cells that are adapted to their function.

Write down the name of two different types of cells, one from plants and one from animals and describe how they are adapted to their function:

Name of plant cell...

How they are adapted to their function ....

.... (2)

Name of animal cell..

How they are adapted to their function ....

.... (2)

3. Using a straight line, link the description on the left to the name of the appropriate process on the right.

| Moving air in and out of the lungs |

| Removal of undigested waste from the gut |

| Particles moving from an area of high concentration to an area of low concentration |

| The release of an egg from the ovary |

| Ovulation |

| Excretion |

| Egestion |

| Fertilisation |

| Diffusion |

| Respiration |

| Breathing |

(4)

4. One food chain found in the woods is:

Hazel nuts ⟶ **Squirrels** ⟶ **Owls**

(a) What does the arrow in the food chain represent?

.... (1)

(b) Which one of the organisms is the predator?

.... (1)

(c) Describe as fully as you can how a producer obtains its food.

....

....

....

.... (2)

(d) Due to a disease, this year the number of owls have fallen dramatically.

Explain fully how this will have an effect on the number of:

Squirrels ....

....

....(2)

Hazel bushes...

....

....(2)

5. John wanted to test the hypothesis that light was needed for photosynthesis.

(a) Complete the equation for photosynthesis below:

Light

.... + ... $\longrightarrow$ .... + ... (2)

(b) John covered a leaf with black strip paper, as shown in the diagram below and then tested the leaf for the products of photosynthesis.

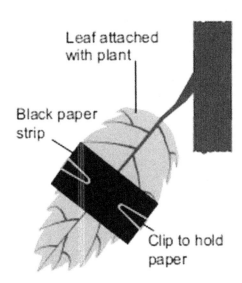

Leaf attached with plant

Black paper strip

Clip to hold paper

(i) Explain why John covered the leaf with a black paper strip.

.... (1)

(c) In order to test for the products of photosynthesis, John follows these 4 steps.

Next to each step explain why these are necessary.

(i) Place leaf in boiling water ....

.... (1)

(ii) Place leaf in warm ethanol ....

.... (1)

9

(iii) Dip leaf in warm water ....

.... (1)

(iv) Cover the leaf in iodine solution ....

.... (1)

(d) Give one safety precaution John must take when performing this experiment.

.... (1)

(e) Draw a labelled diagram below to show what results John would expect when completing his experiment.

(2)

6. Animals have evolved to adapt to the environment they are in. Both polar bears and camels have certain attributes that make them well adapted to the conditions in which they live. For each animal identify two characteristics and describe how it helps them survive.

(i) polar bear characteristic 1

....

how it helps them survive

....

.... (2)

(ii) polar bear characteristic 2

....

how it helps them survive

....

.... (2)

(iii) camel characteristic 1

....

how it helps them survive

....

.... (2)

(iv) camel characteristic 2

....

how it helps them survive

....

.... (2)

7. Elizabeth breathed out into a small beaker of water using a straw and measured the pH of the solution by connecting the solution to an electronic pH meter. She recorded the pH at various intervals and the results are shown below:

Time (s)	pH
0	7.0
5	6.9
10	6.3
15	5.8
20	5.6
30	5.4
40	5.2
50	5.0
60	5.0

(a) Plot these results on the grid below and draw a line of best fit through these points.

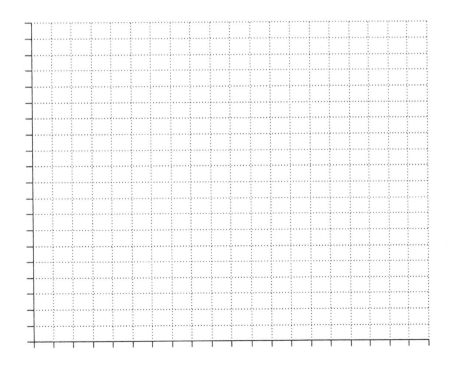

(4)

(b) Describe the results of this experiment.

....

....(2)

(c) Suggest a suitable control for Elizabeths experiment to make this a fair test.

....

....

....(2)

(d) (i) Suggest which gas Elizabeth breathes out could cause the pH to decrease

....   (1)

(ii) Describe a test you could carry out to test your suggestion, including what you would expect to see if the test was positive

....

....(2)

(Total = 60 marks)

SURNAME …………………………….. FIRST NAME ……………………………………….

JUNIOR SCHOOL ………………………….. SENIOR SCHOOL……………………………………..

Avicenna Education ©

COMMON ENTRANCE EXAMINATION AT 13+

SCIENCE

BIOLOGY PRACTICE PAPER 2

Date…………………………………..

Please read the information below before the examination starts.

- The examination is 40 minutes long.

- All answers should be written on the question paper

- Answer **all** questions.

- Calculators are allowed and may be required.

---

1. Underline the option which best completes each of the following sentences:

(a) A group of similar cells form

tissue　　**organs**　　**organ system**　　**organism**

(b) Genes control the production of

carbohydrate　　**protein**　　**DNA**　　**fat**

(c) Amylase is an example of an enzyme which breaks down starch into

glycogen　　**simple sugars**　　**protein**　　**fat**

(d) Fats are an energy source but are also needed for

growth　　**insulation**　　**repair**　　**respiration**

(e) Root hair cells are adapted to their function as they have a

large surface area　　**small surface area**　　**make food**　　**have chloroplast**

(f) An egg cell is an example of a

gamete　　**zygote**　　**fertilization**　　**reproduction**

(g) Ovulation is the name of the process given to the

the fusion of the egg and sperm cell　　**release of an egg from the ovary**

release of sperm　　**formation of the zygote**

(h) An example of a habitat is

freshwater pond　　**herbivore**　　**sunlight**　　**predator**

(i) Antibiotics are medicines used to treat

viral disease　　**scurvy**　　**bacterial disease**　　**athlete's foot**

2. Jack is training for the annual school marathon. He is training to improve the efficiency of his respiration.

(a) Complete the word equation for respiration below:

.... + ... → .... + ... + ...
                                                                                                    (2)

(b) Glucose is an important molecule that we obtain from food. It is found in foods such as rice and pasta which are rich in starch. Explain as fully as you can how glucose is transported into the bloodstream after eating a meal rich in starch.

....

....

.... (3)

(c) As part of training, Jack eats a healthy balanced diet. Name the food group and an example of that food group that Jack will need for growth and repair after an intense training session:

food group   ....

example of food   .... (2)

(d) Jack also abstains from smoking and excessive amounts of alcohol. Give three harmful complications from smoking and excessive intake of alcohol:

1.   ....

2.   ....

3.   .... (3)

3. The diagram below shows the female reproductive system.

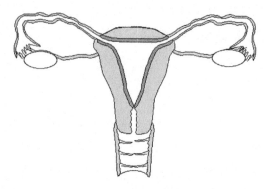

(a) On the diagram above label the **uterus, ovary, vagina** and **fallopian tube.** (2)

(b) Where does fertilization take place? .... (1)

(c) A woman's body mass increases during pregnancy. The table below shows the average increase in mass during pregnancy.

Part	Increase in mass in kg
Uterus	1.0
Placenta	0.8
Foetus	3.7
Amniotic fluid	0.9
Fat	4.0
Red blood cells	0.3

(i) Suggest why the mass of the placenta increases as the foetus develops.

....

....

.... (2)

(ii) Suggest a reason, using the table above, as to why women often need iron supplements during pregnancy.

....

.... (1)

(d) The foetus and the placenta are not part of a woman's body before she becomes pregnant. Which **two** other parts from the table are not present in a woman's body before she becomes pregnant?

.... (1)

(e) The foetus grows inside the amniotic sac, a cavity filled with fluid called amniotic fluid.

Fetus in Utero

(i) Suggest how the amniotic sac and the fluid inside help the foetus survive.

....

.... (2)

(ii) The placenta is a complex structure containing blood vessels of both the mother and the foetus running side by side.

Explain how the foetus receives its food supply from the mother.

.

....

....

....

.... (4)

(iii) If a pregnant woman inhales smoke from a cigarette, carbon monoxide can bind to her red blood cells. How could this harm the foetus?

....

.... (1)

4. Bacteria that develop resistance to antibiotics are growing problem in hospitals. One example is the MRSA bacteria pictured below:

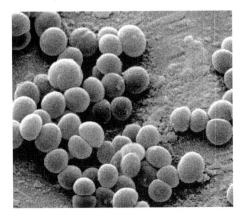

(a) When MRSA reproduce they pass on this resistance. Which part of the cell is responsible for passing on this information?

.... (1)

(b) Pathogens, such as MRSA, can spread in hospitals from person to person.

Suggest two ways in which this can happen.

1. ....

2. .... (2)

(c) Some people can become immune to certain disease by being vaccinated.

Describe how vaccination can prevent a person from getting disease.

....

....

....

.... (3)

5. There are five classes of vertebrates.

(a) Complete the table below which shows the type and characteristics of each class of vertebrate.

Vertebrate Class	Characteristic
....	Dry, scaly skin
amphibian	....
....	Obtain oxygen using gills
birds	....
....	Suckles young on milk

(5)

(b) State three characteristics of an insect.

1. ....

2. ....

3. .... (3)

6. The diagram below shows the bones and muscles of a human arm.

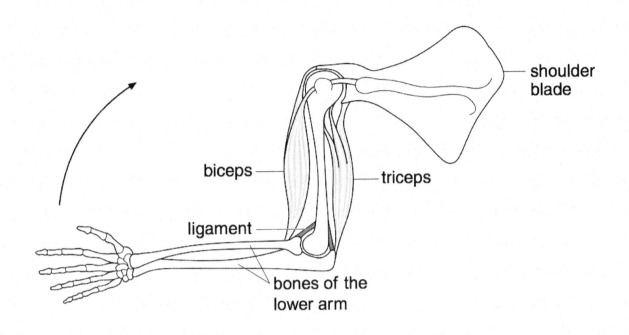

(a) On the diagram above label where the **tendons** are. (1)

(b) Why is it important that the tendons don't stretch during contraction?

....

.... (1)

(c) Ligament hold bones together at a joint and can stretch. Why is it important for ligaments to be able to stretch?

....

.... (1)

(d) The ends of the bones are covered in a layer of smooth cartilage and contain synovial fluid. Why are they required in a joint?

....

.... (1)

7. A group of year 9 pupils prepared and viewed some of their cheek cells using a microscope.

(a) Describe how you would prepare your own cheek cells to be viewed under the microscope.

....

....

....

.... (4)

(b) Describe and explain how you would use the microscope to view the cheek cells you had prepared.

....

....

.... (2)

(c) Cells taken from the skin of an animal were examined under a microscope and were found to have 28 chromosomes.

How many chromosomes would be present in the female gamete?

.... (1)

(d) In the table below tick only **one** box next to each human characteristic as to whether it is **inherited only**, or **inherited and affected by the environment.**

Human Charecteristic	Inherited only	Inherited and affected by the environment
Height		
Eye colour		
Weight		
Skin colour		

(2)

(Total = 60 marks)

SURNAME …………………………….....   FIRST NAME ……………………………………..

JUNIOR SCHOOL ……………………………   SENIOR SCHOOL…………………………………….

Avicenna Education ©

COMMON ENTRANCE EXAMINATION AT 13+

SCIENCE

CHEMISTRY PRACTICE PAPER 1

Date…………………………………...

Please read the information below before the examination starts.

- The examination is 40 minutes long.

- All answers should be written on the question paper

- Answer **all** questions.

- Calculators are allowed and may be required.

1. Underline the option which best completes each of the following sentences:

(a) Air consists mostly of

oxygen   **carbon dioxide**   **nitrogen**   **hydrogen**

(b) the name for the reaction between hydrochloric acid and sodium hydroxide is

precipitation   **neutralization**   **displacement**   **decomposition**

(c) the best method for separating water from a mixture of sand and water is

chromatography   **filtration**   **evaporation**   **distillation**

(d) an oxide which has a pH value greater than 7 is

carbon dioxide   **sulphur dioxide**   **magnesium oxide**   **water**

(e) the gas given off when magnesium is added to dilute hydrochloric acid is

carbon dioxide   **nitrogen**   **helium**   **hydrogen**

(f) A substance has a melting point of -70° C and a boiling point of 72° C. At -80° C the substance will be

a solid   **a liquid**   **a gas**   **a solution**

(6)

2.

| mercury | hydrogen | water | helium |
| carbon | carbon dioxide | | |

From the box above, use ONE substance which best describes the descriptions below. It should be assumed that all substances are at room temperature.

(a) is a gaseous compound ....

(b) produced when zinc is mixed with acid..

(c) is a noble gas ....

(d) good conductor of electricity...

(e) a liquid compound ....

(f) When burnt in oxygen, produces a substance which turns limewater cloudy

....

(6)

3. The graph below shows how the solubilities of three salts changes with temperature.

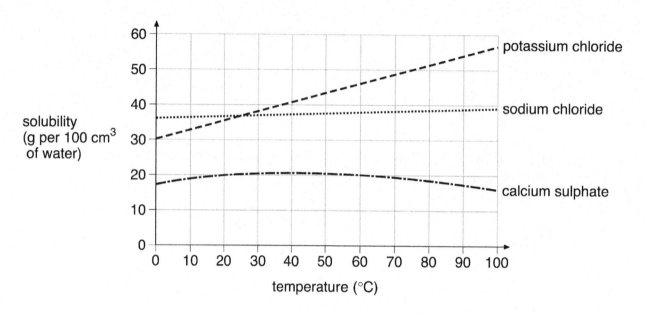

(a) Using the graph, compare the solubility of potassium chloride and sodium chloride

....

....

.... (2)

(b) Jessica put 50g of potassium chloride into a beaker with $100cm^3$ of water at 90°C.

What would you expect to happen to the potassium chloride?

....

.... (1)

(c) She then cooled the beaker down to room temperature. What would she see in the beaker? Explain your answer.

....

....

.... (2)

(d) The water in a small lake had the three salts mentioned above dissolved in it. During a very warm summer the water had evaporated leaving the salts in the order shown below:

potassium chloride

sodium chloride

calcium sulphate

Using the graph suggest what temperature you think these salts were deposited at? Explain your reason.

....

....

.... (2)

4. Samantha used chromatography to identify the different coloured substances in the ink from her felt-tip pen. To do this she used three coloured ink dyes, green, blue and purple as well as her felt-tip pen. She used water as the solvent.

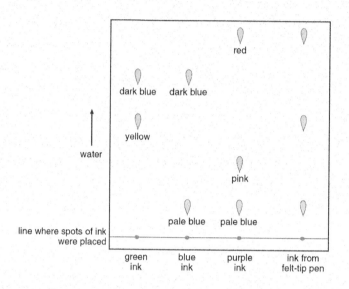

(a) Using the diagram above, which colours were present in Samantha's felt-tip pen?

....

.... (1)

(b) How many substances were present in the purple ink? Explain your answer.

....

.... (2)

(c) Samantha was unsure as to whether to se a felt-tip pen or a pencil to draw the line where the spots of ink were placed. Which one should she use? Explain your answer.

....

....

.... (2)

(d) Samantha used water as the solvent in this experiment. Jack attempted to repeat the experiment with a different set of pens but it did not work. He then tried the experiment with ethanol as the solvent instead of water and it worked. Suggest why the experiment worked with ethanol but not with water.

....

.... (1)

(e) Chromatography is one way to separate substances. Other mixtures must be separated in different ways. Describe how you would separate a mixture of iron filings, salt and chalk.

....

....

....

....

....

.... (4)

5. A group of student placed three metal wires in different salt solutions as shown below:

experiment	1	2	3
diagram	copper wire silver nitrate solution	zinc wire lead nitrate solution	copper wire lead nitrate solution
observations	crystals of silver formed on the wire	crystals of lead formed on the wire	no change

(a) Using the table above write the order of the reactivity of the four metals lead, silver, copper and zinc.

most reactive ....

....

....

least reactive ....

(2)

(b) Complete the word equation for the reaction in test tube 1.

silver nitrate + copper → .... + ... (2)

(c) One of the pupils then dipped a fresh piece of a metal wire into hydrochloric acid. This reacted with the acid.

   (i) Which metal was this?

.... (1)

   (ii) What would you observe when this metal reacted with hydrochloric acid?

.... (1)

   (iii) How would you test for the observation in part (ii)

.... (1)

(d) One of the pupils hypothesized that there would be no reaction between a zinc wire and silver nitrate solution. Was he correct? Explain your answer.

....

.... (2)

(e) Gold is never found combined with other elements naturally. Where would you place gold in part (a)? Explain your answer.

....

.... (2)

6. (a) To be considered a fuel what must a substance release when it is burnt?

.... (1)

(b) Most of the fuels used in today's society come from 'fossil fuels'.

   (i) How are these fossil fuels formed?

   ....

   .... (2)

   (ii) Give an example of a fossil fuel.

   .... (1)

(c) Nitrogen makes up the majority of the gas in the air. Under normal conditions it is very unreactive. However, atmospheric nitrogen can react with atmospheric oxygen in a lightning storm or in a car engine. Explain why?

   ....

   ....

   .... (2)

(d) Many fossil fuels contain sulfur as an impurity. How can the presence of sulfur lead to the production of acid rain when the fuel is burnt?

   ....

   ....

   .... (2)

(e) The acid rain formed from the oxides of nitrogen and sulfur can damage various materials. Depending on the type of material they damage, they give off different gases.

Acids can react with metals to give off a flammable gas. Complete the equation below:

sulfuric acid   +   iron   →   iron sulfide + ... (1)

7. Sodium and chloride are two different elements in the periodic table with different physical and chemical properties.

(a) Complete the table below:

Element	Chemical symbol	Physical state at room temperature
Sodium		
Chlorine		

(3)

(b) Describe three physical properties that show that sodium is a metal.

....

....

.... (3)

(c) Chlorine is a very toxic gas. What safety precautions would the teacher need to take if this was used in the laboratory?

....

.... (2)

(d) When sodium is ignited and placed in a jar of chlorine a violent reaction takes place with the formation of a white solid.

(i) What is the name of this white solid?

.... (1)

(Ii) Is this an element, compound or mixture?

.... (1)

(iii) This reaction also gives off a lot of heat. What is the name given to reaction that give off heat?

.... (1)

(Total = 60 marks)

SURNAME .... FIRST NAME ....

JUNIOR SCHOOL .... SENIOR SCHOOL................................

Avicenna Education ©

COMMON ENTRANCE EXAMINATION AT 13+

SCIENCE

CHEMISTRY PRACTICE PAPER 2

Date.......................................

Please read the information below before the examination starts.

- The examination is 40 minutes long.

- All answers should be written on the question paper

- Answer **all** questions.

- Calculators are allowed and may be required.

1. Underline the option which best completes each of the following sentences:

(a) A substance which contains only one type of atom is

oxygen   **water**   **magnesium oxide**   **calcium carbonate**

(b) a substance which turns limewater milky is

hydrogen   **oxygen**   **carbon dioxide**   **nitrogen**

(c) in a salt solution, the salt is the

solute   **filtrate**   **solvent**   **residue**

(d) when calcium carbonate is heated, the following reaction occurs:

calcium carbonate → calcium oxide + carbon dioxide

This reaction is an example of

reduction   **decomposition**   **combustion**   **neutralization**

(e) the pH of the stomach is roughly

2   **6**   **7**   **9**

(f) an element which forms an acidic oxide is

gold   **carbon**   **silver**   **copper**

(6)

2. Air is a mixture of many gases, some of which are shown below

Name	Chemical Formula
nitrogen	N_2
oxygen	O_2
argon	Ar
carbon dioxide	CO_2

(a) Which of these gases are:

(i) elements ………………………………………………………….

(ii) compounds…………………………………………………….. (2)

(b) What is the average percentage of carbon dioxide in the air?

………………………………………………………………………. (1)

(c) The amount of carbon dioxide in the air varies from place to place. The amount of carbon dioxide in the countryside is often lower than in towns and cities. Explain why.

………………………………………………………………………………………..

………………………………………………………………………………………..

…………………………………………………………………………………… (2)

(d) Judy performed an experiment to find out how much oxygen there was in the air.

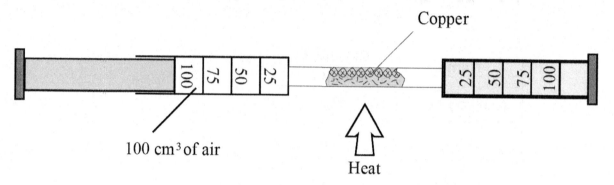

Copper

100 cm³ of air

Heat

The 100cm³ of air was pushed from the syringe on the left to the syringe on the right over hot copper, repeated several times.

(i) complete the word equation below which shows how oxygen was removed:

copper + oxygen → ....   (1)

(ii) The surface of the copper changed colour when it was heated as air was passed over it.

The colour before heating was ....

The colour after heating was ....   (2)

(iii) What volume of the air would you expect to be left in the syringe at the end of the experiment.?

....   (1)

(iv) Why was an excess of copper used in this experiment?

....

.... (1)

3. Susan investigated differences between chemical and physical changes. She put three chemicals in separate cubicles and weighed each one. She heated the crucible and then weighed each crucible again after they had cooled down.

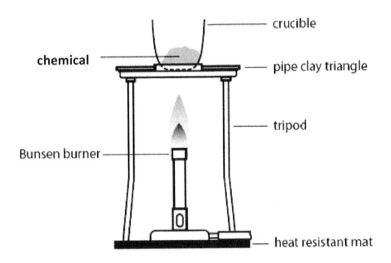

Her observations are recorded in the table below:

Experiment	chemical	observation	Change in mass
A	magnesium (silver solid)	Burned brightly in air and formed a white powder	....
B	zinc oxide (white powder)	Turned pale yellow on heating and then turned white again on cooling	no change
C	potassium permanganate (purple crystals)	The crystals turned black with a colourless gas given off	decrease

(a) In experiment A, magnesium reacts with a gas present in the air. Complete the equation below.

magnesium + ………………………… → …………………………   (2)

(b) What change in mass would you expect in experiment A? Explain your answer.

………………………………………………………………………………………………

………………………………………………………………………………… (2)

(c) The gas given off in experiment C re-lit a glowing split. What is the name of this gas?

………………………………………………………………………………… (1)

(d) What was the name of the white powder left at the end of experiment B?

………………………………………………………………………………… (1)

(e) In each of the experiments above, did a chemical or a physical change occur?

Tick one box for each experiment.

Experiment	chemical	physical
A		
B		
C		

                                                                    (2)

4. Copper carbonate is placed in a test tube and heated until it has completely reacted. A black solid and a colourless gas is produced. The gas is then made to react with limewater as shown below:

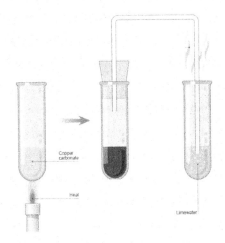

(a) What is the name given to this type of reaction.

.... (1)

(b) What is the name of the black solid?

.... (1)

(c) The product reacts with limewater and you conclude that the gas is carbon dioxide.

(i) What is the chemical formula for carbon dioxide?

.... (1)

(ii) How many atoms are there in carbon dioxide?

.... (1)

(iii) Give two observations that support your conclusion that is carbon dioxide.

....

.... (2)

5. Jeremy set up an experiment to investigate the rusting of iron. He set up five experiments as shown below and left the test tubes for four days.

| A | B | C | D | E |
| iron nail in distilled water | iron nail in tap water which has been boiled to remove dissolved gases | iron nail and a chemical to absorb water vapour | iron nail in sea water | iron nail in vinegar |

He wrote down all of the results in the table below:

Test tube	Observation
A	Nail slightly rusty
B	Nail still shiny
C	Nail still shiny
D	....
E	Nail slightly rusty, bubbles of gas forming

(a) What would you expect to see in test-tube D? Explain your answer.

....

.... (2)

(b) Why had the nail in test tube B still remain shiny and not rust?

....

.... (1)

(c) In test tube E the iron nail was placed in vinegar.

(i) Is vinegar acidic, neutral or alkaline? ……………………………………… (1)

(ii) Suggest the name of the gas formed in this test tube.

……………………………………………………………………………………… (1)

(d) What is the chemical name given to rust?

……………………………………………………………………………………… (1)

(d) Jeremy weighed the nail in test tube D before the experiment. He then re-weighed the nail with the rust (after drying it out) after the four days. What change, if any, would you expect? Explain your answer.

………………………………………………………………………………………

………………………………………………………………………………………

………………………………………………………………………………………

……………………………………………………………………………… (2)

6. The diagrams below show the arrangement of molecules or atoms in five different substances A, B, C, D and E.

Each of the circles ⬤, ◯ and ⚫ represents an atom of a different element.

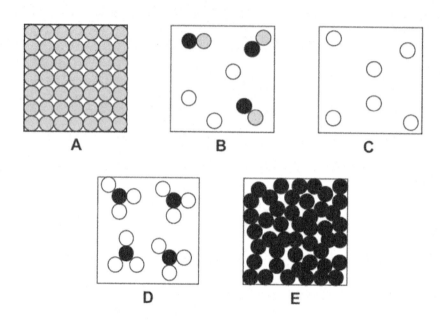

A   B   C

D   E

(a) Which letter or letters represents the following:

(i) a mixture of gases..

(ii) a single compound ....

(iii) an element ....   (3)

(b) Below is a diagram which shows a model of a chemical reaction between two substance.

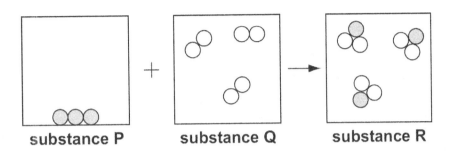

substance P   substance Q   substance R

(i) Using the diagram, how can you tell that a chemical reaction has taken place between substance P and substance Q?

....

.... (1)

(Ii) Substance P is carbon. Suggest what the substance Q and R could be.

substance Q ....

substance R ....   (2)

(c) Using the diagram, explain how it shows that the mass has been conserved in this reaction.

....

.... (1)

7. Ellen was comparing the strength of three different acids **A**, **B** and **C**. In each case she dropped a 1cm strip of magnesium ribbon into a beaker containing $25cm^3$ of each acid. She then measured the time taken for the magnesium to react completely:

Acid	Time taken (s)
A	26
B	12
C	60

(a) State two ways in which Ellen carried out a fair test

1: ....

2: .... (2)

(b) Suggest two other ways in which Ellen could have ensured that this was a fair test.

1: ....

2: .... (2)

(c) Stat two safety precautions that Ellen should use.

1: ....

2: .... (2)

(d) Using Ellen's results which of the three acids do you think is the strongest? Explain your answer.

....

.... (2)

(e) Suggest another way in which Ellen could identify the strongest acid.

.... (1)

(f) Citric acid is found in oranges and dissolves in water. Elllen tried to separate the citric acid from the water using filtration. Explain in terms of particles, why this method of separation would not work.

....

.... (2)

(g) Ellen decided to try simple distillation to obtain the acid instead. Draw a labeled diagram of the apparatus which she could use.

(3)

(h) Ellen found that her distillate was pure water instead of acid. Suggest why this might be.

.... (1)

(Total = 60 marks)

SURNAME ....   FIRST NAME ....

JUNIOR SCHOOL ....   SENIOR SCHOOL.....................................

COMMON ENTRANCE EXAMINATION AT 13+

SCIENCE

PHYSICS PRACTICE PAPER 1

Date...................................

Please read the information below before the examination starts.

- The examination is 40 minutes long.

- All answers should be written on the question paper

- Answer **all** questions.

- Calculators are allowed and may be required.

---

1. Underline the option which best completes each of the following sentences:

(a) a form of energy which describes a ball rolling on the floor is

friction   **sound**   **kinetic**   **thermal**

(b) the unit of a moment is

m   **N**   **cm**   **Nm**

(c) sound does not travel through

a liquid   **a solid**   **a gas**   **a vacuum**

(d) an object has a mass of 70kg.On Mars where gravity exerts a force of 3.5N on 1kg, the weight of the object will be

70 N   **245 N**   **140 N**   **350 N**

(e) Draw lines to join the picture on the left to the correct symbol on the right.

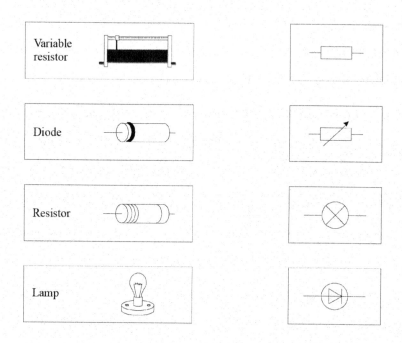

(6)

2. Jacob wanted to find out the density of air. He set up the experiment as shown below:

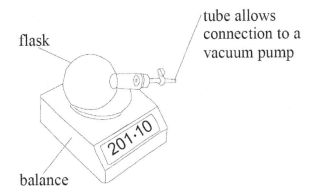

The flask was initially weighed filled with air. Jacob then connected the flask to a vacuum pump so that all the air was sucked out and weighed the empty flask.

(a) What is the formula relating density, mass and volume?

…………………………………………………………………………………………… (1)

(b) As a safety precaution the teacher placed a screen between the flask and the students. Why must a safety screen be used in this experiment?

……………………………………………………………………………………………

…………………………………………………………………………………………… (1)

(c) In order to work out the density of air, Jacob needs to know the volume of the flask.

Suggest how he could find the volume of the flask.

……………………………………………………………………………………………

……………………………………………………………………………………………

…………………………………………………………………………………………… (2)

(d) Jacob's results are below:

Volume of flask: 1200cm^3

Mass of flask and air: 202.65g

Mass of empty flask: 201.10g

(i)   Calculate the mass of the air in the flask.

.... (1)

(ii)   Calculate the density of the air in the flask.

....

....

.... (2)

(e) Helium is often used to fill balloons that are used in a balloon race.

Explain why helium is used rather than air to fill the balloons.

....

.... (1)

(f) The diagram below shows how the volume of a fixed mass of helium gas changes as the pressure is changed.

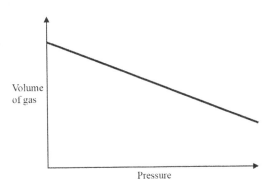

(i) What other factor can affect the volume of a fixed mass of helium gas?

.... (1)

(ii) Describe how the volume of gas changes as the pressure is increased.

....

....

.... (2)

3. A father makes a simple toy for his son, using plastic animals (an elephant and a monkey) as shown below:

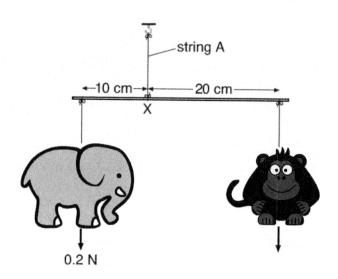

(a) The elephant weighs 0.2 N What is the turning moment produced by the elephant about point X? Give the correct units.

....

.... (2)

(b) The toy is balanced. What is the turning moment produced by the monkey about point X?

....

.... (1)

(c) What is the weight of the monkey?

.... N   (1)

(d) What is the size of the tension force of string A?

.... N   (1)

4. Elephants keep themselves cool by losing heat from their ears.

African Elephant   Asian Elephant

(a) Using the pictures above, suggest which elephant has the ability to lose more heat from its ears. Give a reason for your answer.

....

....

.... (2)

(b) Rosie filled two conical flasks with 300cm^3 of hot water. In each conical flask she placed a piece of metal strip to model the elephants ears as shown below:

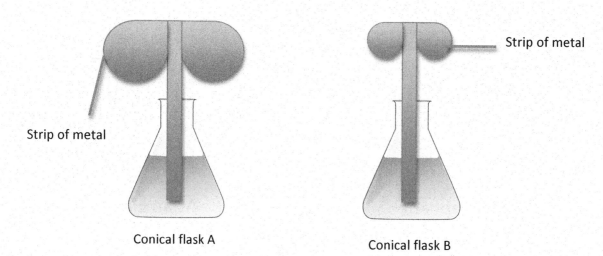

Strip of metal

Strip of metal

Conical flask A

Conical flask B

She then recorded the temperature of the water in the conical flask every 5 minutes using a thermometer, as shown below:

time (minutes)	Temperature ($^\circ$C)	
	Flask A	Flask B
0	60	60
5	53	56
10	49	53
15	45	51
20	42	49
25	39	47

(i) Give two ways in which Rosie made her test fair.

1: ....

2: .... (2)

(ii) Plot the results for flask A and B in the graph below and draw lines of best fit.

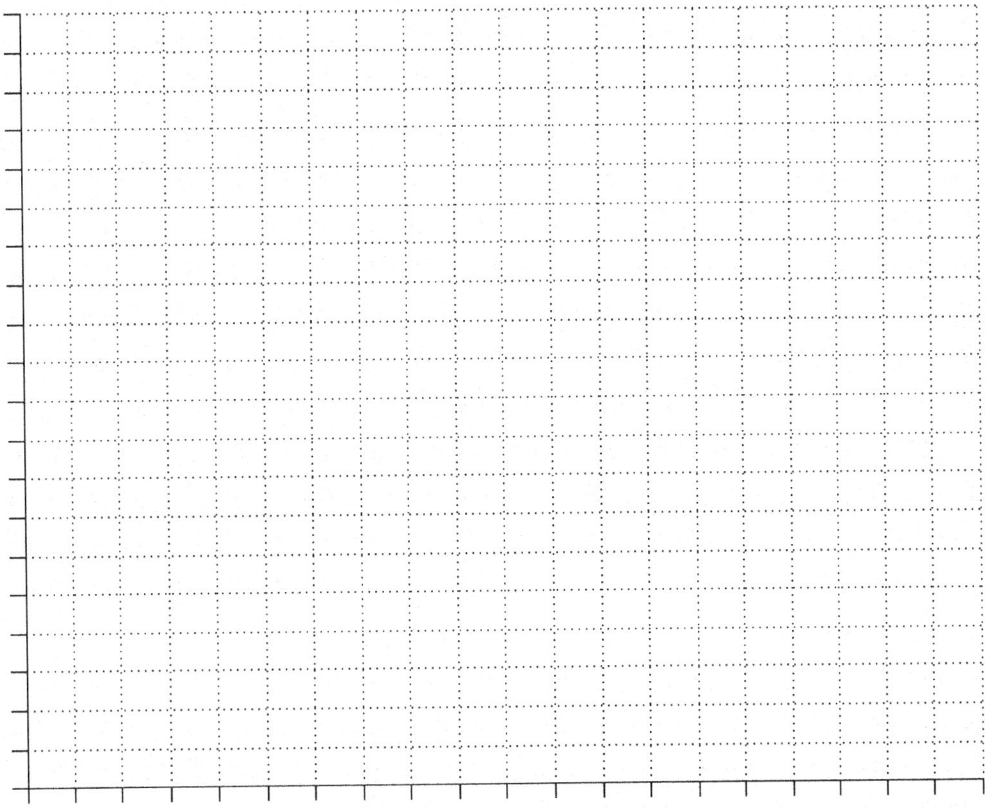

(4)

(iii) Why do you think it is more useful to present Rosie's findings in a graph rather than a table?

....

.... (1)

(c) In what way do Rosie's results agree or disagree with your answer to part (a)?

....

....

.... (2)

(d) Rosie repeated the experiment, but used a temperature sensor and a data logger to record her results. Give two advantages to this.

1: ....

2: .... (2)

(5) Complete the following sentences using words from the box below:

thermal	**kinetic**	**electrical**	**light**
sound	**gravitational**	**chemical**	

Jack connects a generator called a dynamo to his bicycle. When he pedals his bicycle, the back wheel turns the generator.

As Jack pedals, ……………………….. energy in his muscles gets converted to kinetic energy. When the generator turns, this kinetic energy then gets changed to

……………………….. energy in the wires. This energy is then converted to useful

…………………….. energy in the bulb. However, some of the energy in the bulb is

wasted as ……………….. energy.

(4)

(6) The rear window of a car contains a heating element as shown below, which is connected to the battery of the car in a circuit.

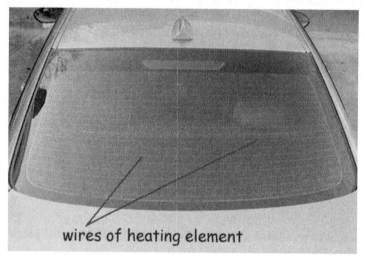

wires of heating element

The diagram below demonstrates two different ways of connect the circuit of a heating element:

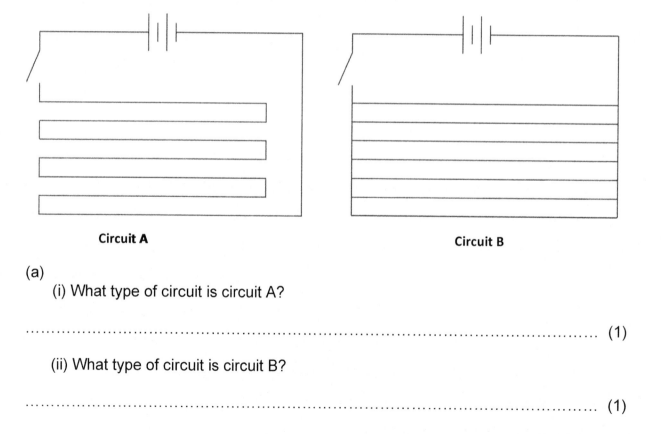

Circuit A   Circuit B

(a)
   (i) What type of circuit is circuit A?

.... (1)

   (ii) What type of circuit is circuit B?

.... (1)

(b) Part of the wire in circuits A and B get broken at points P and Q as shown below

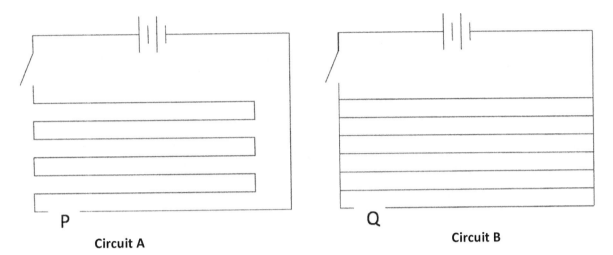

Circuit A   Circuit B

When the switch is closed how does it affect the heating element in

    (i)   circuit A?

....

.... (1)

    (ii)   circuit B?

....

.... (1)

7. The table below gives information about the planets in the Solar System, listed in alphabetical order.

planet name	average distance from the Sun /million km	diameter /km	time for one orbit round the Sun	time for one rotation on its axis /hours	temperature on surface of planet /°C
Earth	150	13 000	365 days	24	+22
Jupiter	780	140 000	12 years	9.8	−150
Mars	230	6800	687 days	25	−23
Mercury	58	4900	88 days	1400	+350
Neptune	4500	51 000	165 years	16	−220
Pluto	5900	2300	248 years	150	−220
Saturn	1400	120 000	29 years	10.2	−180
Uranus	2900	51 000	84 years	17	−210
Venus	110	12 000	225 days	5800	+480

(a) Explain why Pluto and Neptune are the coldest planets in our Solar System.

....

.... (1)

(b) Explain why there could be no liquid water on the surface of Mars **and** Venus.

....

....

.... (2)

(c) Which planet has the shortest time between sunrise and sunset?

.... (1)

(d) Which planet has the shortest year?

.... (1)

(e) Name the force which keeps the planets in orbit.

.... (1)

(f) Mars takes nearly twice as long as Earth to fully orbit the Sun. Venus takes significantly less time than Earth to fully orbit the Sun. The diagram below shows the position of the three planets at one particular time where all three planets were lined up with the Sun:

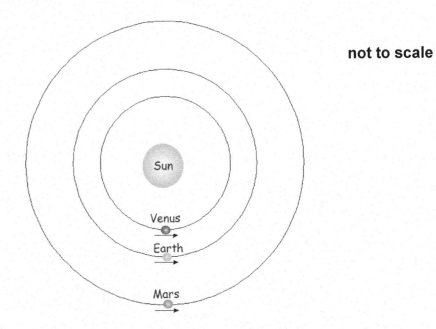

not to scale

(i) On the diagram, show the position of the Earth three months after the planets were lined up, using the letter E.

(1)

(ii) On the diagram show the approximate position of Mars three months after the planets were lined up, using the letter M. Explain why Mars is in this position.

....

.... (2)

8. Lodestone is a magnetic rock, and was commonly used by travellers as a compass. They floated the rock on a piece of wood and placed it in a small bowl of water.

   (a) (i) Why was it necessary for them to float the lodestone?

   .... (1)

   (ii) In what way would this help the travellers navigate their way?

   ....

   .... (1)

   (b) On the diagram below draw lines to show the magnetic field pattern around the bar magnet. Include the direction of the field using arrows:

                                                                                    (2)

   (c) An electromagnet can be made from a coil of wire wound round an iron core. When the current flows through the wire, it forms an electro magnet.

   (i) State two ways in which an electromagnet can be made stronger.

   1: ....

   ....

   2: ....

   .... (2)

(ii) State one use of a large electromagnet.

.... (1)

(iii) Give one advantage of an electromagnet compared to a bar magnet.

.... (1)

(Total = 60 marks)

SURNAME ………………………………….. FIRST NAME ……………………………………….

JUNIOR SCHOOL ………………………….. SENIOR SCHOOL…………………………………

Avicenna Education ©

COMMON ENTRANCE EXAMINATION AT 13+

SCIENCE

PHYSICS PRACTICE PAPER 2

Date………………………………..

Please read the information below before the examination starts.

- The examination is 40 minutes long.

- All answers should be written on the question paper

- Answer **all** questions.

- Calculators are allowed and may be required.

1. Underline the option which best completes each of the following sentences:

(a) An example of a renewable energy source is

coal   **oil**   **solar power**   **gas**

(b) An energy **efficient** light bulb will reduce the amount of energy transferred as

light   **sound**   **thermal**   **kinetic**

(c) A cheetah runs 160m in 8 seconds giving it a speed of

2m/s   **20m/s**   **200m/s**   **10m/s**

(d) The speed of an object moving at a constant speed can be maintained by

keeping the forces acting on it the same   **increasing the force acting on it**
decreasing the force acting on it   **applying an additional force on it**

(e) the time taken for Jupiter to orbit the Sun

takes longer than the time taken for Earth to orbit the Sun

is shorter than the time taken for Earth to orbit the Sun

is the same as the time taken for Earth to orbit the Sun

is longer than the time taken for Pluto to orbit the Sun

(f) if the amplitude of the sound from a guitar is increased, the sound will be

higher pitched   **lower pitched**   **louder**   **quieter**

(6)

2. Michael uses a battery (two cells), one light bulb and a switch to make a series circuit.

(a) (i) Draw Michael's circuit diagram and label the components.

(3)

(ii) Michael connects another bulb to his circuit in series. Explain what would happen to the current in his new circuit compared to the current in the circuit in part (i).

....

....

.... (2)

(b) A corridor has a switch at each end, with a light bulb in the middle as shown in the diagram below:

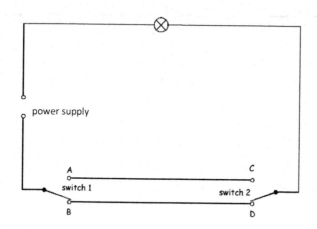

Complete the table below to show whether the light bulb is on or off. The first row has been done for you.

Position of switch 1	Position of switch 2	Light bulb ON or OFF
B	D	ON
A	D	
B	C	
A	C	

(3)

(c) The corridor has been refurbished and now has two light bulbs, one at each end as shown in the diagram below.

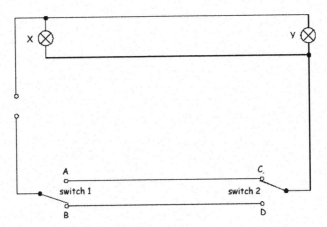

(i) In the diagram above, which bulbs, if any, are lit?

.... (1)

(ii) The switches are then flicked so that both bulbs are lit. Bulb Y breaks. What, if anything, happens to bulb X?

.... (1)

3. The diagram below shows a lighthouse and three boats moored in the water at night time.

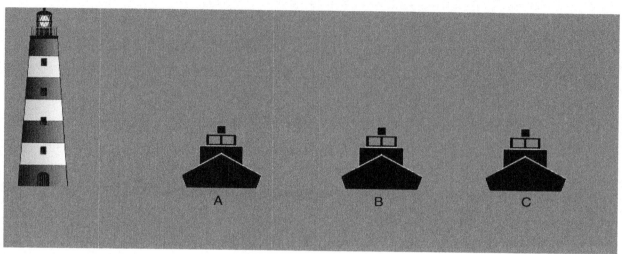

(a) On which boat A, B, or C would the light from the lighthouse be the brightest?

.... (1)

(b) Each boat makes a shadow on the water. Draw a 'X' on the diagram to show where the shadow of boat A will be. Explain why a shadow forms there.

....

.... (2)

(c) Inside the lighthouse there is a powerful lamp and several mirrors. The diagram shows a lamp and a mirror inside the lighthouse.

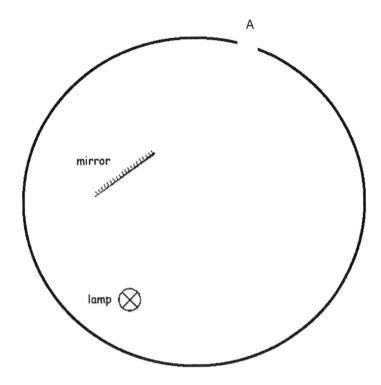

On the diagram draw carefully to show:

    (i)   the path of the light ray which reaches the mirror.

    (ii) the path of the light ray which leaves the mirror.   (3)

(d) What is the name of the process which occurs when light strikes the mirror?

....   (1)

(e) Draw a second mirror in the diagram, at the correct angle so that the light ray will come out at point A. Show the path which this light takes.

                                                                                               (2)

4. On 11th August 1999 there was a total solar eclipse visible from the UK.

(a) The diagram below shows the Moon and the Earth. On the diagram draw where the Sun must be and shade in the region on Earth where the eclipse is taking place:

Moon

Earth

(2)

(b) In the sky the moon looks about the same size as the Sun, although the Sun is much larger. Suggest a reason for this.

....

.... (1)

(c) The map below shows the shape of the moon's shadow and the path it takes across Cornwall.

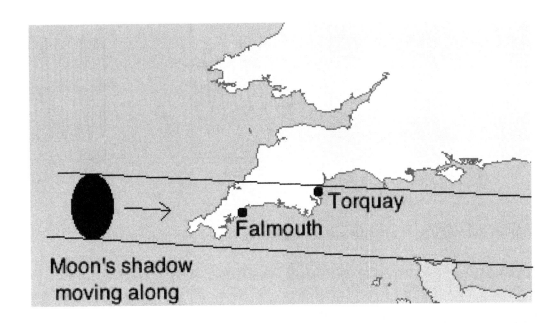

(i) Give two reasons as to why the Moon's shadow moves over the surface of the Earth?

1: …...

2: …... (2)

(ii) The moon's shadow takes approximately 2 minutes to move across a house in Falmouth but takes less than 2 minutes to cross over a house in Torquay. Suggest a reason for this.

…...

….. (1)

5. The diagram below shows three sound waves as seen by an oscilloscope.

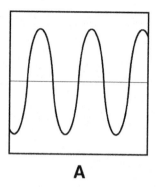
A

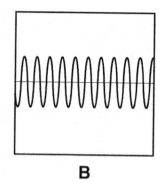
B

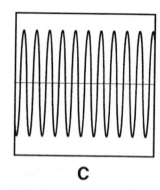
C

(a) Which two waves have the same loudness? Explain your answer.

....

.... (2)

(b) Which two waves have the same pitch? Explain your answer.

....

.... (2)

(c) Jonathan listens to a song that produces the pattern below.

X 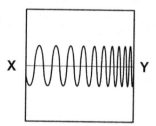 Y

Describe how the sound changes between X and Y.

.... (1)

Avicenna Education ©

(d) Explain what happens to the human ear drum as the sound gets louder.

....

.... (1)

(e) The astronauts who landed on the Moon needed to wear special spacesuits which were filled with air, because there is a vacuum in the Moon. In order to speak to each other they needed to communicate via radios which were **inside** the helmet.

(i) Explain why sound doesn't travel on the Moon.

....

.... (1)

(ii) If the radios broke, the astronauts could put their helmets together so they touched. They could then hear each other's voices. Suggest a reason why.

....

.... (1)

6. Susan is standing some distance from a large cliff, where she shouts her name and hears the echo.

(a) What word is given to the process by which echo's occur?

.... (1)

Susan uses her watch to time how long it takes for her to hear the echo. She is standing 90 metres from the cliff and finds that it takes 0.7 seconds.

(b)

(i) State the equation which relates speed, distance and time.

.... (1)

(ii) Using the data above, calculate the speed of sound in air.

....

....

.... (2)

(c) Explain why her measurement is not very accurate.

.... (1)

(d) Suggest two ways in which Sue could improve the accuracy of her measurements using the **same** method.

1: ....

....

2: ....

....(2)

7. Jamie investigates the stretching of a spring. He uses a set of 1N weights and measures and records how much the spring stretches for each weight.

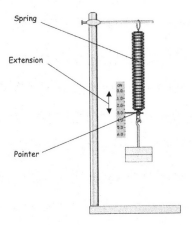

(a) The scale does not start at the top of the spring. Suggest why.

....

....

.... (2)

Jamie's results are shown in the table below.

Weight added in N	Position of pointer in cm
1	1.6
2	
3	4.7
4	6.9
5	7.5

(b) From the diagram, read off the position of the pointer for a weight of 2N and add this reading to the table.

(1)

(c) On the graph grid below,

    (i) label both axes and add suitable scales (2)

    (ii) plot the data points (2)

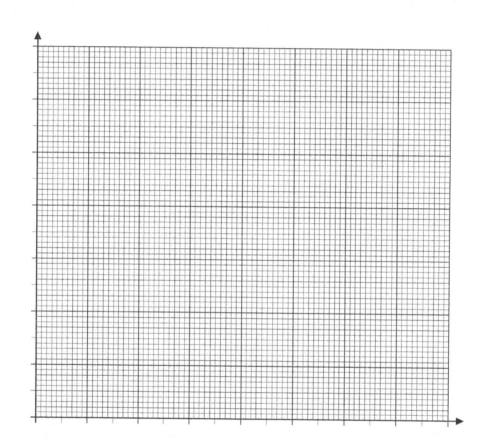

(d) One of the readings in the table seems incorrect

   (i) Suggest which reading this may be

.... (1)

(ii) What should Jamie do about this reading.

....

.... (1)

(e) Draw a line of best fit to your graph. (1)

(f) Using the graph describe the relationship between the weight and the extension of the spring and the name of the 'Law' given to this relationship.

....

.... (2)

(g) Jamie takes the weight off the spring and attaches a stone to the spring. The pointer points to the 6cm mark.

(i) Use your graph to find the **mass** of the stone.

(Assume the Earth exerts a gravitational force of 10N/kg)

....

.... (2)

(Total = 60 marks)

CPSIA information can be obtained
at www.ICGtesting.com
Printed in the USA
BVOW09s0842071116
467120BV00004B/132/P